I0541478

I AM

A FAITH BASED AFFIRMATION

ACTIVITY JOURNAL
for Girls

BY : KAYLA JONES

A NOTE TO PARENTS/GUARDIANS

Welcome to my debut book!

As parents, guardians, and mentors, you undoubtedly recognize the significance and importance of nurturing a strong foundation of faith in the hearts of your children. I have created this affirmation activity journal with that exact intention in mind. This isn't just a journal for young readers, it is hopefully an opportunity for meaningful and deep conversations about Jesus. Every page has been crafted to captivate and challenge the reader, hopefully igniting curiosity about what it means to have faith while learning how they can be more confident in their self-worth.

I am a mother to four boys, and I want two main things for children to remember as they go about their day: ONE – God's unwavering love for them, TWO – Their self-worth. I feel that affirmations are reminders of how God feels about us, we are loved because he first loved us. Believing the affirmations or truths about yourself can change the trajectory of your mood and how we interact with one another. My goal was to introduce affirmations to young minds in a biblical way, so that they can understand how the two go hand in hand.

This journal was designed for children who can read and write on their own and those who have a love for being creative. With a grown ups help, younger children will be able to complete the activities as well. I hope this journal can serve as a tool for your child to grow in their faith so that they can know just how special and unique they are, created in God's image.

Cheerfully in Christ,

Kayla Jones

P.S. Stay connected with me on Instagram @kaylajonesart to see what I am up to!

THINGS ABOUT ME

I AM

YEARS OLD

THIS JOURNAL BELONGS TO :

_____

MY FAVORITE ACTIVITIES ARE :

WHEN I GROW UP I WANT TO BE :

MY FAVORITE FOODS ARE :

I AM HAPPIEST WHEN :

MY FAVORITE SUBJECT IN SCHOOL IS :

MY FAVORITE BOOKS ARE :

MY FAVORITE TV SHOW OR MOVIE IS :

MY FAVORITE COLOR IS :

MY SELF PORTRAIT

I AM LOVED

LOVE THE LORD YOUR GOD WITH ALL YOUR HEART AND WITH ALL YOUR SOUL AND WITH ALL YOUR MIND AND WITH ALL YOUR STRENGTH. — MARK 12:30

I FEEL LOVED WHEN :

I SHOW LOVE BY :

PRAYER : Loving Father, may you help me to love others as You have loved me, with compassion and care. Amen.

COLOR IN THE WAYS THAT YOU LIKE TO BE SHOWN LOVE.

WHEN SOMEONE SHARES A SPECIAL TREAT WITH YOU.

WHEN YOU ARE GIVEN HUGS AND KISSES.

WHEN A GROWN UP LISTENS TO YOU TELL A STORY.

WHEN YOU ARE GIVEN A NEW TOY.

WHEN YOU ARE TOLD HOW AMAZING YOU ARE.

WHEN YOU ARE TOLD THAT YOU ARE LOVED.

WHEN SOMEONE DOES AN ACTIVITY WITH YOU.

FREE DOODLE

USE THIS PAGE TO DOODLE SOMETHING FUN THAT HAPPENED TODAY OR HOW YOU ARE FEELING.

I AM CAPABLE

IN THE SPACES BELOW WRITE SOMETHING THAT YOU WANT TO LEARN HOW TO DO.

EXAMPLE: I WANT TO LEARN HOW TO FLY A KITE BY MYSELF.

PRAYER : Lord, please help me remember that I can do hard things and give me courage when I try. Thank you for making me capable and strong. Amen.

BELIEVE IN YOURSELF

MY DREAM BUCKET LIST

FREE DOODLE

USE THIS PAGE TO DOODLE SOMETHING FUN THAT HAPPENED TODAY OR HOW YOU ARE FEELING.

Philippians 4:13

I can do ALL THINGS through CHRIST who gives me STRENGTH.

I AM BEAUTIFUL

Beauty isn't just about how you look on the outside, like your colorful clothes or the way you style your hair. It's also about how you treat others with kindness and how you believe in yourself. When you are happy and kind, that special sparkle of yours makes you truly shine, and that's what makes you beautiful in every way!

ALWAYS REMEMBER, YOU ARE BEAUTIFUL BOTH ON THE INSIDE AND THE OUTSIDE!

Look in the mirror, what do you see that you like? Is it your sparkling eyes, your pretty smile? What 3 things do you like most about yourself?

Write them here.

_____

_____

_____

PRAYER : Lord, thank you for making me so uniquely me. Help me to see the beauty that surrounds me as I go about my day. Amen.

Ask a grown up if you can have old magazines and newspapers. With their permission cut out words or phrases that describe you. Things you like about yourself and words that describe how special you are. Use a glue stick to paste the words below.

Examples : FUN - CREATIVE - SILLY - AWESOME - SMILING

FREE DOODLE

USE THIS PAGE TO DOODLE SOMETHING FUN THAT HAPPENED TODAY OR HOW YOU ARE FEELING.

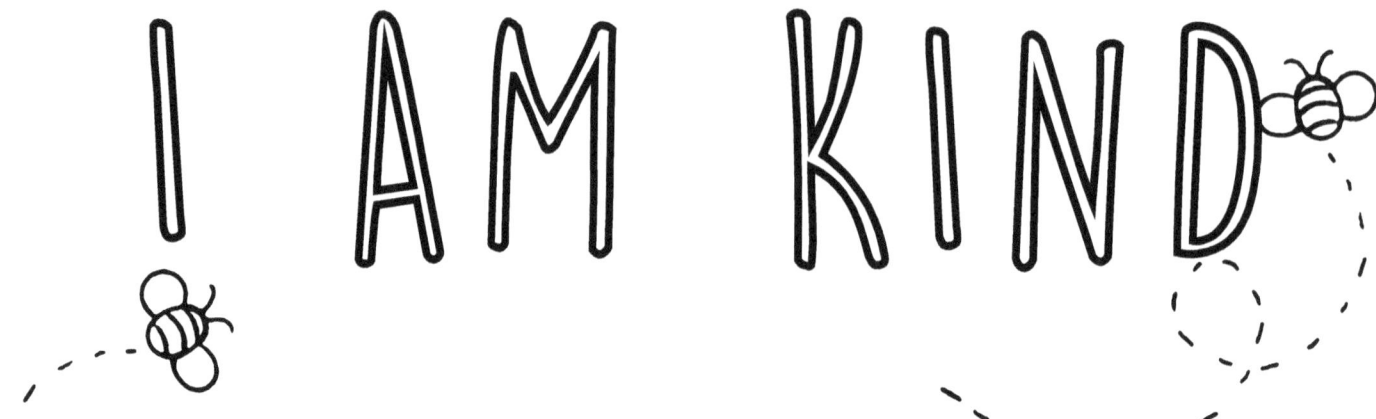

I AM KIND

ACTS OF KINDNESS

An ambassador is someone who is a positive representative of a group or a place. You can become an ambassador for your community by doing small acts of kindness in your everyday routines.

Color in the acts of kindness that you want to do the next time you are out in your community.

HOLD THE DOOR OPEN FOR SOMEONE

TEACH A YOUNGER CHILD SOMETHING YOU ARE GOOD AT

HELP WITH YARD WORK

HELP CARRY IN GROCERIES

PUT MONEY IN THE OFFERING AT CHURCH

DONATE A TOY THAT YOU NO LONGER PLAY WITH

GIVE SOMEONE A COMPLIMENT

WRITE A POSITIVE MESSAGE IN CHALK ON YOUR SIDEWALK

SAY THANK YOU WHEN YOU ARE AT A RESTAURANT

TAKE OUT THE TRASH

PRAYER : Lord, fill my heart with kindness so that I can spread love wherever I go in life – both in big and small ways! Will you please show me how I can be a blessing to others. Amen.

FILL THESE JARS WITH
IDEAS OF HOW YOU CAN
SHOW KINDNESS TO
OTHERS.

FREE DOODLE

USE THIS PAGE TO DOODLE SOMETHING FUN THAT HAPPENED TODAY OR HOW YOU ARE FEELING.

Kind words are like HONEY sweet to the SOUL

Proverbs 16:24

HONEY

I AM HONEST

WHAT IS INTEGRITY?

Integrity is like being a superhero for your heart and actions. It means always doing the right thing, even when no one is watching. Imagine you have a special compass inside you that guides you to make honest and fair choices. It's important because it helps you build strong friendships, gain the respect of others, and feel proud of yourself. Just like how superheroes use their powers for good, having integrity helps you make the world a better place by making good choices and treating everyone with kindness.

Remember, being true to yourself and doing what's right, even when it's hard, is what makes you a true integrity superhero!

- -

PRAYER : Thank you for guiding me each day. Please help me to be honest, kind and true in everything I say and do. Amen.

I HAVE INTEGRITY !

WRITE A FEW WAYS THAT YOU CAN SHOW INTEGRITY.

EXAMPLE : BEING HONEST WHEN YOU ARE ASKED IF YOU CLEANED YOUR ROOM.

FREE DOODLE

USE THIS PAGE TO DOODLE SOMETHING FUN THAT HAPPENED TODAY OR HOW YOU ARE FEELING.

I AM STRONG

OVERCOMING FAILURE

Failing is actually a super important part of learning and growing. It is normal to fail sometimes, and it happens to everyone. When we try again after failing, we become even stronger and smarter. It's like when you try a new puzzle and some pieces don't fit at first. But you keep trying and soon enough you find the right piece that fits perfect. Those little failures teach us valuable lessons that will make us stronger.

Think about a time that you failed at something. How did it make you feel? How did you overcome it?

— —

PRAYER : Lord, please help me to stay positive and focused on the good things in life, no matter what challenges come my way. Amen.

CALMING STRATEGIES

Sometimes it can be frustrating to fail. Do you know what it is to be frustrated? Frustration is feelings of anger, sadness and even scared when there is a problem or struggle. It's that feeling when you might feel a bit stuck or a little upset because things aren't going smoothly.

HERE ARE A FEW EXERCISES TO TRY THE NEXT TIME YOU FEEL THESE BIG EMOTIONS.

COUNT TO 20 SLOWLY

DRAW A PICTURE OF SOMETHING THAT MAKES YOU HAPPY

LOOK IN THE MIRROR AND MAKE SILLY FACES AT YOURSELF

PUT ON HAPPY MUSIC AND DANCE IT OUT

TAKE 10 DEEP BREATHS

DO SOME STRETCHES

THINK OF A CALMING STRATEGY THAT WILL HELP YOU THE NEXT TIME YOU FEEL FRUSTRATED.

FREE DOODLE

USE THIS PAGE TO DOODLE SOMETHING FUN THAT HAPPENED TODAY OR HOW YOU ARE FEELING.

I AM CREATIVE

Creativity can mean different things to different people! Just like how you might like to draw colorful pictures, someone else might like to write poetry or make up cool dance moves. Just like an artist creates beautiful paintings, God used His creativity to make our incredible Earth. God is the ultimate artist by giving us colorful sunsets and sunrises, tall trees that change colors, flowers with brightly colored petals and big fluffy clouds that dance.

REMEMBER, CREATIVITY IS ALL ABOUT USING YOUR IMAGINATION TO MAKE WONDERFUL THINGS, JUST LIKE GOD DID WITH OUR AMAZING WORLD!

PRAYER : God, thank you for making the world so colorful and full of wonders. Help me to use my creativity to see the magic in everyday things. Thank you for sharing your creativity with the world. Amen.

On a day with big fluffy clouds ask a grown up if you can take a blanket outside to look up at the clouds. When you are laying down, looking up at the clouds think about how they mold into different shapes. Use your imagination to form creatures and objects. Write down what you saw in the cloud doodles below.

CLOUD CREATIONS

FREE DOODLE

USE THIS PAGE TO DOODLE SOMETHING FUN THAT HAPPENED TODAY OR HOW YOU ARE FEELING.

I AM FAITHFUL

After the great flood, God made a promise to Noah and all humanity, that he would never again flood the earth. God gave us a rainbow in the sky as a sign of his promise to Noah and for all generations to come. It serves as a reminder of God's great love for us.

When we see rainbows today, we know that every rainbow is still a sign of the promise made thousands and thousands of years ago between God and all generations of humanity. We can trust that God will remain faithful to his promise and never again flood the earth. God made a powerful promise strong in grace, love, and forgiveness. The rainbow reminds us that we can trust God's faithfulness no matter what we are going through.

"I have set my rainbow in the clouds, and it will be the sign of the covenant between me and the earth. Whenever I bring clouds over the earth and the rainbow appears in the clouds, I will remember my covenant between me and you and all living creatures of every kind. Never again will the waters become a flood to destroy all life" (Genesis 9:13-15)

PRAYER : Lord, I want to stay close to you and be faithful every day. Show me the path of kindness and patience, and help me make good choices. Thank you for always being there for me. Amen.

FRUIT OF THE SPIRIT

Did you know that Faithfulness is a fruit of the spirit found in the bible. The fruit of the Spirit, found in Galatians 5:22-23, is made up of nine qualities or gifts:

LOVE   JOY   PEACE   PATIENCE   KINDNESS

GOODNESS   FAITHFULNESS   GENTLENESS   SELF CONTROL

With the help from a grown up, lets make a treat, celebrating the fruits of the spirit.

FRUIT PIZZA

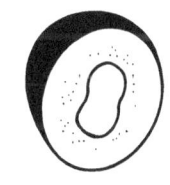

Ingredients

* 1 (16 oz) tube refrigerated sugar cookie dough
* 1 (8 oz) pkg cream cheese, softened
* 2 Tbsp butter, softened
* 1 tsp vanilla extract
* 2 cups powdered sugar
* Fruits that you enjoy, sliced

Instructions

*Preheat oven to 350 degrees.

*On pizza pan or cookie sheet press your cookie dough into about a 12" circle.

*Bake for about 10-15 minutes or until slightly golden, remove and let cool.

*While the cookie dough is cooling, in bowl mix together your cream cheese, butter, extracts and powdered sugar until combined.

*Spread over cooled cookie crust.

*Top with fruit in a fun design of your choice.

- *Parents, please note that this recipe does not factor in food allergies.*

FREE DOODLE

USE THIS PAGE TO DOODLE SOMETHING FUN THAT HAPPENED TODAY OR HOW YOU ARE FEELING.

I AM LOYAL

Loyalty means being true and faithful to your friends and family, standing up for them when they need you. Just like your favorite teddy bear who is always with you, loyalty is being a true friend and showing love no matter what happens.

Describe a time when someone was loyal to you.

How did it make you feel?

Write about a time when you were loyal.

PRAYER : God, thank you for my friends and family who are always there for me. Help me learn what it means to be loyal. Help me to stand up for the things I believe in and to be trustworthy. Amen.

TRUST AND LOYALTY

Just like two puzzle pieces fit together, trust and loyalty fit together to create strong and successful relationships.

Trust is when you believe that someone will do what they say, this is called reliable. Loyalty, is when you stick by someone no matter what and support them. It's like being a good friend even when things are tough.

When you trust someone, you're more likely to be loyal to them because you know they won't let you down. When you are loyal, you are showing that you believe in the other person.

HOW CAN I SHOW GOD THAT I AM LOYAL AND TRUST HIM?

By allowing God to remind you who He is and what He promises us all. It is important to be honest with Him. You can tell God how you feel and in what areas of your life you are struggling to trust Him.

FREE DOODLE

USE THIS PAGE TO DOODLE SOMETHING FUN THAT HAPPENED TODAY OR HOW YOU ARE FEELING.

We Have THIS HOPE AS AN ANCHOR for the SOUL, FIRM AND SECURE.

Hebrews 6:19

I AM SMART

Intelligence is having a super amazing brain that can think, learn, and understand lots of things. It's not just about knowing facts, but also about being able to figure out puzzles, solve problems, and come up with really cool ideas. Everyone's intelligence is unique, so remember that being smart doesn't mean knowing everything – it means using your brain to explore and discover new things in your own special way.

ASSIGN A DIFFERENT COLOR TO EACH FOOD ITEM. COLOR AND COUNT HOW MANY OF EACH FOOD TYPE THERE IS IN THE PICTURE BELOW AND WRITE THE NUMBER IN THE SPACE BY THE PICTURE.

PRAYER : Dear God, help me see that I am smart and important, with unique talents to share. Thank you for believing in me, and please remind me to believe in myself too. Amen.

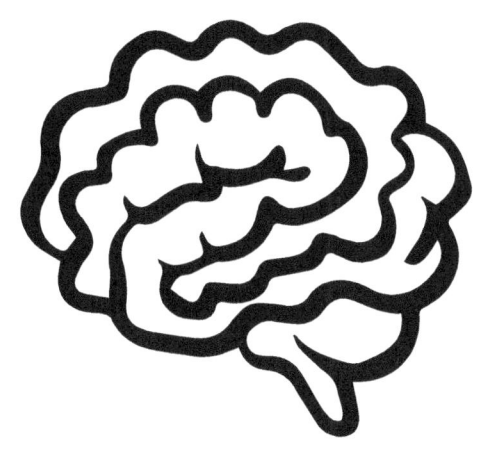

Sometimes we all need a brain break. Color in the brain break ideas that look like fun to you and try them out the next time you need to rest your brain for a moment.

COUNT HOW LONG YOU CAN STAND ON ONE FOOT WITHOUT NEEDING TO PUT YOUR OTHER FOOT DOWN.

PICK ANY COLOR. NOW FIND AS MANY THINGS IN THE ROOM THAT ARE THIS COLOR AND SAY THEM OUT LOUD.

BUILD SOMETHING AS TALL AS YOU CAN WITH LEGOS OR BLOCKS.

MAKE AIR SHAPES

IN THE AIR WITH YOUR FINGER DRAW THESE OBJECTS:

A HAPPY FACE

MOON AND STARS

TREES

CLOUDS

WAVES IN THE OCEAN

MAKE UP A SILLY SONG AND SHARE IT WITH YOUR FAMILY.

FREE DOODLE

USE THIS PAGE TO DOODLE SOMETHING FUN THAT HAPPENED TODAY OR HOW YOU ARE FEELING.

I AM BOLD

BOLDNESS IN FAITH

When you are bold in your faith, the love you have for Jesus shines so that all can see. Being bold may mean you share stories about Jesus with your friends, or you might show kindness and love to others, just like Jesus did. It can also simply be inviting a friend to church with you.

Being bold is also about not being afraid to ask questions and learn more about your faith. This is how we grow closer to God. Remember, being bold in your faith doesn't mean you won't have doubts sometimes, but facing those doubts and challenges with courage can make your faith even stronger.

Be bold in your faith as you go about your day and share the love of Jesus!

THINK OF WAYS
YOU CAN
BE BOLD
IN YOUR FAITH.

Write them here →

PRAYER : Lord, please give me courage and strength to be bold even when I'm afraid. Help me remember that you're always by my side, and with you, I can face anything. Thank you for being my source of strength. Amen.

GOD USES ORDINARY PEOPLE WHO ARE {BOLD} TO DO AMAZING THINGS!

Having the courage to ask questions about God is being BOLD in your faith.

Write down a few questions that you have about faith. Then discuss these questions with someone that you trust.

QUESTIONS THAT I HAVE

FREE DOODLE

USE THIS PAGE TO DOODLE SOMETHING FUN THAT HAPPENED TODAY OR HOW YOU ARE FEELING.

I AM HELPFUL

LIST THE WAYS THAT YOU ARE HELPFUL IN YOUR ...

SCHOOL

HOME

CHURCH

COMMUNITY

PRAYER : Dear God, help me be a shining light of kindness and love in the world. Show me how to share, listen, and care for my friends and family. Amen.

GIVE A HELPING HAND

WRITE DOWN WAYS YOU CAN BE HELPFUL TO OTHERS.

1.

2.

3.

FREE DOODLE

USE THIS PAGE TO DOODLE SOMETHING FUN THAT HAPPENED TODAY OR HOW YOU ARE FEELING.

LET ALL THAT YOU DO BE DONE IN LOVE.

1 Corinthians 16:14

I AM FRIENDLY

WHAT IT MEANS TO BE A FRIEND

Friends support each other, cheer each other up, and respect each other's feelings. It means being kind, listening when they talk, and sharing both good times and bad times with them.

THINK OF WAYS YOU CAN BE A GOOD FRIEND....

Example: Sharing your snack with your friend when they don't have one.

PRAYER : Lord, thank you for the friends that you have given me. Help me to be a good friend and show them love and appreciation every day. Amen.

THEREFORE ENCOURAGE ONE ANOTHER AND BUILD EACH OTHER UP, JUST AS YOU ARE DOING.

— 1 THESSALONIANS 5:11

Think about your friends, write down what you like about them and how they make you feel.

NAME :

NAME :

NAME :

NAME :

FREE DOODLE

USE THIS PAGE TO DOODLE SOMETHING FUN THAT HAPPENED TODAY OR HOW YOU ARE FEELING.

I AM
TALENTED

I AM GOOD AT :

I AM PROUD OF MYSELF WHEN :

PRAYER : Lord, thank You for all the wonderful gifts You have given me, please help me appreciate my talents and use them to glorify you. Amen.

Did you know that even the most talented people in the world have to practice so they can get better? Just like when you learn to ride a bike or play a new game, practice helps you get better and better. Remember, practice makes your skills shine bright, just like a star in the sky!

IN THE STARS, WRITE DOWN SOMETHING THAT YOU ARE TALENTED AT AND HOW YOU CAN PRACTICE TO GET BETTER.

EXAMPLE

TALENT : Basketball

Practice for 30 minutes every day.

TALENT :

TALENT :

TALENT :

FREE DOODLE

USE THIS PAGE TO DOODLE SOMETHING FUN THAT HAPPENED TODAY OR HOW YOU ARE FEELING.

I AM SPECIAL

Write something that made you feel special each day.

SUNDAY

MONDAY

TUESDAY

WEDNESDAY

THURSDAY

FRIDAY

SATURDAY

PRAYER : God, thank you for making me just the way that I am. Help me remember that I am precious in your eyes and that your love shines on me every day. Amen.

MY JOY JAR

Ask a grown up if you can have a jar and some paper or sticky notes. We are going to make a JOY JAR! Each time someone or something brings you joy or makes you feel special write it down. Then fold up the paper and place it in your jar so that when you feel sad or angry you can pull the paper from your joy jar and read about all the times that you felt special.

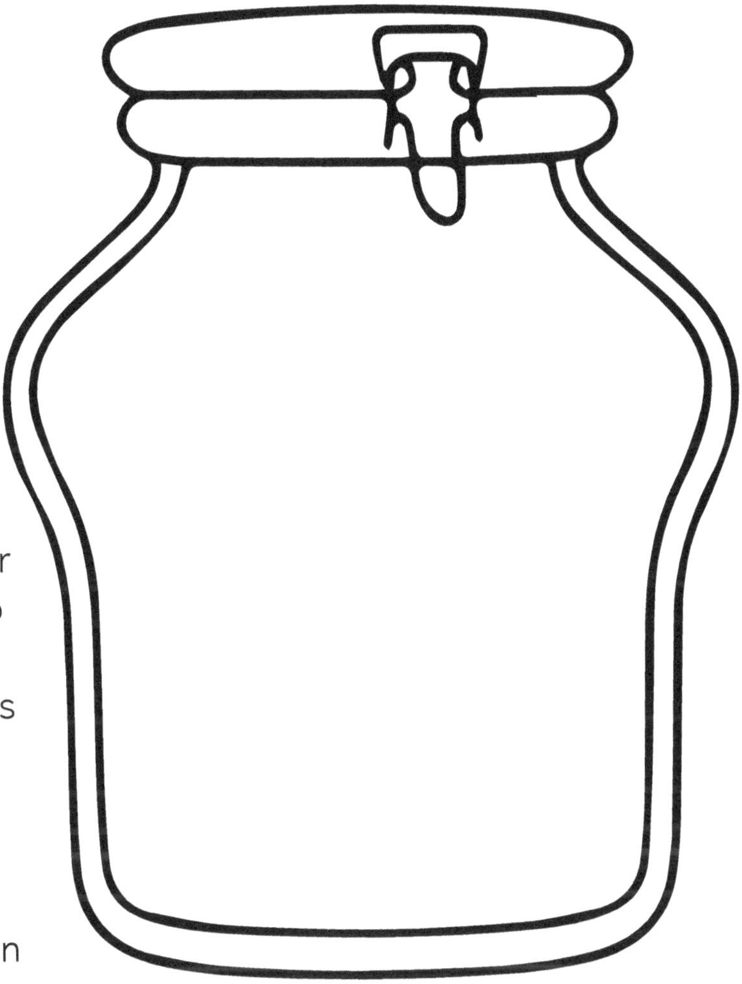

FREE DOODLE

USE THIS PAGE TO DOODLE SOMETHING FUN THAT HAPPENED TODAY OR HOW YOU ARE FEELING.

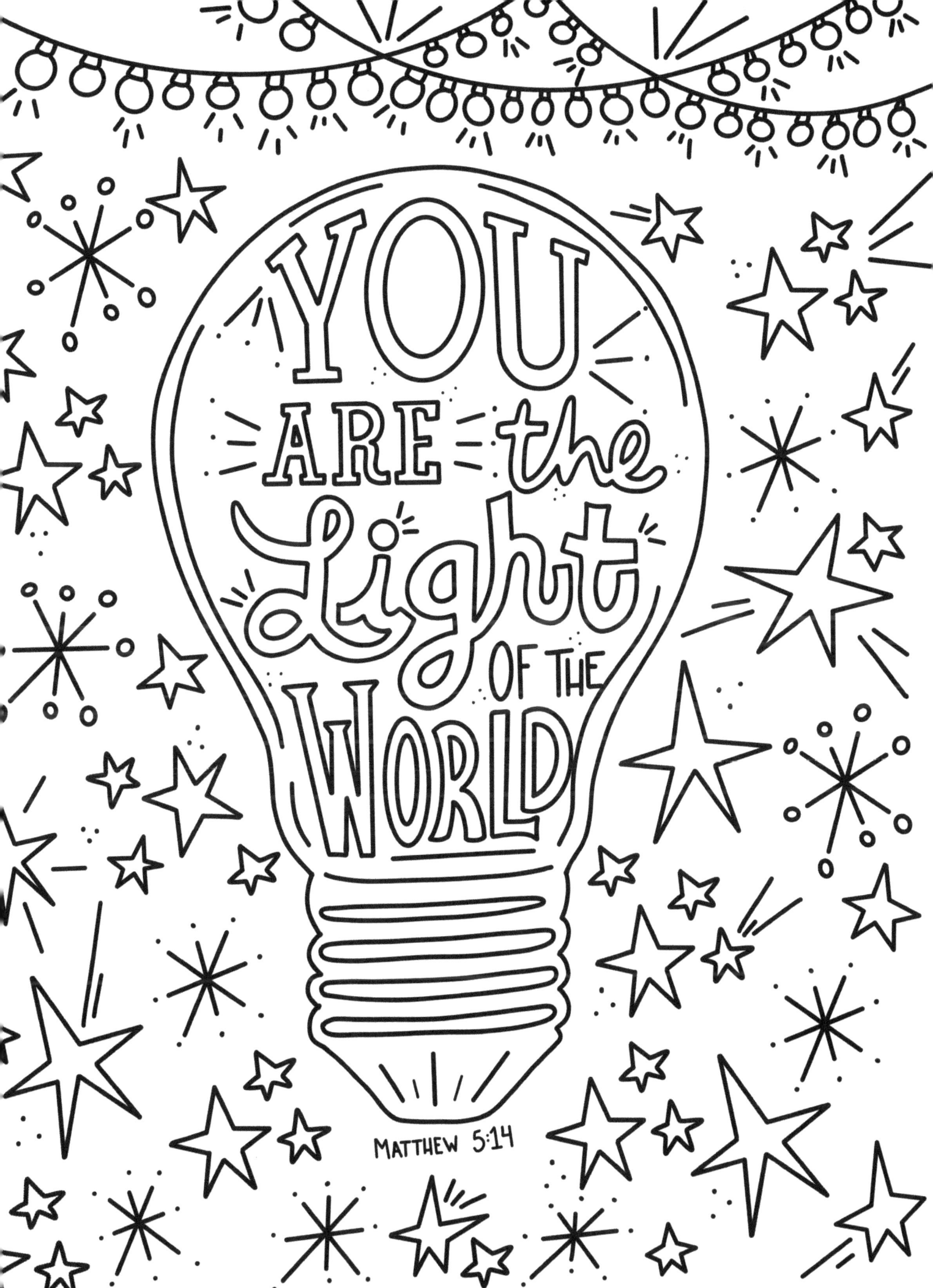

I AM BRAVE

CONFIDENCE

Confidence is when you believe in yourself. It's knowing that you can do things, even if they seem a little hard at first. Just like when you learn to ride a bike, at first it might be wobbly, but the more you practice, the more confident you become that you will stay on the bike. You can have confidence by focusing on your strengths and the things you're good at.

Change your mindset. When something is hard and you think that you can't do something tell yourself.... I can't **YET**, but I will!

FILL OUT THE BANK SPACES BELOW, CHANGING THE MINDSET.

I CAN'T _____ BUT, SOON I WILL.

I DON'T KNOW _____

_____ YET, BUT I WILL LEARN.

I DON'T KNOW HOW TO _____

_____ YET, BUT SOON I WILL KNOW HOW TO.

PRAYER : Dear God, please give me courage to believe in myself and the strength to face any challenge or difficulty that comes my way. Amen.

DARE TO BE BRAVE

This week try to challenge yourself and do something that scares you just a little bit. *(This exercise is to push you to try something new, NOT to put yourself in harm's way.)* Dare yourself to be brave in a situation that you don't normally do. This could include trying a new food, raising your hand in class to answer a question or even trying a new sport that you haven't done before.

REMEMBER, YOU CAN DO HARD THINGS!

IDEAS

- -

- -

- -

- -

FREE DOODLE

USE THIS PAGE TO DOODLE SOMETHING FUN THAT HAPPENED TODAY OR HOW YOU ARE FEELING.

BE STRONG & COURAGEOUS

DO NOT BE AFRAID OR TERRIFIED BECAUSE OF THEM,

FOR THE

LORD YOUR GOD

GOES WITH YOU;
HE WILL NEVER LEAVE YOU

NOR FORSAKE YOU.

Deuteronomy 31:6

I AM IMPORTANT

Do you know how important you are?

Each day you wake up, the world gets a little brighter because you are in it!

You have a special gift – the power to spread joy, kindness, and love to everyone you meet.

Remember, it's not about being the best at everything, but about being the best **YOU** that you can be.

PRAYER : Dear Lord, thank you for loving me just the way I am. Please remind me every day that I matter, and that my thoughts, feelings, and dreams are important. Amen.

WHAT ARE SOME THINGS THAT PEOPLE DO TO MAKE YOU FEEL THAT YOU ARE IMPORTANT? WRITE THEM HERE.

Examples : You are put in charge of a task at school, or when your friends take your advice.

_____

FREE DOODLE

USE THIS PAGE TO DOODLE SOMETHING FUN THAT HAPPENED TODAY OR HOW YOU ARE FEELING.

I AM GRATEFUL

DRAW SOMETHING THAT YOU ARE GRATEFUL FOR TODAY.

PRAYER :

Lord, bless this world, both near and far.
With gratitude like a shining star.
Thank you for all that I receive,
Your steadfast love is why I believe.

 # GRATITUDE SCAVENGER HUNT

☆ FIND SOMETHING THAT MAKES YOU LAUGH

_ _
what made you laugh?

☆ GIVE SOMEONE YOU LOVE A HUG

_ _
who did you hug?

☆ FIND SOMETHING THAT GIVES YOU COMFORT

_ _
what was it?

☆ FIND SOMETHING THAT MAKES YOU FEEL SAFE

_ _
what makes you feel safe?

☆ FIND SOMETHING OUTSIDE YOU ENJOY DOING.

_ _
what is it?

☆ HELP SOMEONE DO A TASK

_ _
what was the task?

FREE DOODLE

USE THIS PAGE TO DOODLE SOMETHING FUN THAT HAPPENED TODAY OR HOW YOU ARE FEELING.

I AM ENOUGH

We all have different feelings and moods each day. Keep track of what you are feeling each day with this mood chart. Assign a feeling a color and everyday color in the photo with the mood you most felt that day.

⬜ HAPPY ⬜ SAD ⬜ SILLY ⬜ IRRITATED ⬜ EXCITED

PRAYER : Lord, help me remember everyday that your love for me is big and strong. Remind me that I have a special place in this world and that I am enough. Amen.

A to Z amazing

THINGS THAT MAKE ME WHO I AM.

Write something that starts with each letter of the alphabet that describes you and how amazing you are.

A _____

B _____

C _____

D _____

E _____

F _____

G _____

H _____

I _____

J _____

K _____

L _____

M _____

N _____

O _____

P _____

Q _____

R _____

S _____

T _____

U _____

V _____

W _____

X _____

Y _____

Z _____

FREE DOODLE

USE THIS PAGE TO DOODLE SOMETHING FUN THAT HAPPENED TODAY OR HOW YOU ARE FEELING.

DAILY AFFIRMATIONS

TODAY...

I AM
GOING TO MAKE GOOD CHOICES

I AM
THINKING POSITIVE THOUGHTS

I AM
A LEADER

I AM
GOING TO SHOW OTHERS KINDNESS AND LOVE

I AM
A HELPER

I AM
GOING TO TRY MY BEST

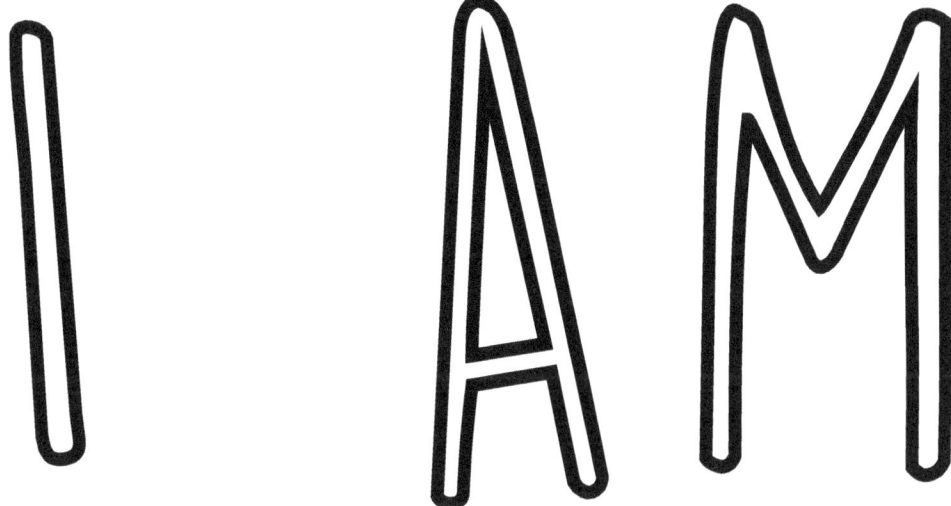

I AM

- -

WRITE YOUR OWN AFFIRMATION.

PRAYER : Thank you for this day and for all the good things in my life. Please watch over my family and family. Help me be kind, brave, and make good choices in everything I do. Amen.